READING POWER

Biomes

Tundra

Holly Cefrey

The Rosen Publishing Group's
PowerKids Press™
New York

Published in 2003 by The Rosen Publishing Group, Inc.
29 East 21st Street, New York, NY 10010

First Edition

Book Design: Mindy Liu

Photo Credits: Cover © Paul A. Souders/Corbis; p. 4 © Scott T. Smith/Corbis; p. 5 © Darrell Gulin/Corbis; p. 7 © MapArt; p. 8 © William Bernard/Corbis; p. 9 © Galen Rowell/Corbis; p. 10 © Uwe Walz/Corbis; p. 11 © Pat O'Hara/Corbis; p. 12 © Charles Mauzy/Corbis; p. 13 © John Lemker/Animals Animals; p. 14 © W. Perry Conway/Corbis; p. 15 © Shane Moore/Animals Animals; p. 16 (inset) © Dan Guravich/Corbis; pp. 16–17 © Index Stock; p. 18 © Maria Stenzel/National Geographic Image Collection; p. 19 © Farrell Grehan/Corbis; p. 21 © Wolfgang Kaehler/Corbis

Library of Congress Cataloging-in-Publication Data

Cefrey, Holly.
Tundra / Holly Cefrey.
    p. cm. — (Biomes)
Summary: Describes the fragile ecosystem of a tundra.
Includes bibliographical references and index.
ISBN 0-8239-6452-3 (library binding)
1. Tundras—Juvenile literature. [1. Tundras. 2. Tundra ecology. 3. Ecology.] I. Title.
GB571 .C44 2003
577.5'86—dc21

                                    2002000085

Contents

Tundra 4

Arctic Tundra 8

Alpine Tundra 12

Living in the Tundra 16

Glossary 22

Resources 23

Index/Word Count 24

Note 24

Tundra

The tundra biome is a cold, dry region where trees cannot grow. Temperatures can fall to −25 degrees Fahrenheit (−32 degrees Celsius) or lower in tundra regions. There are two types of tundras—arctic and alpine.

Arctic tundra

Alpine tundra

Now You Know

A biome (*BY-ohm*) is a plant and animal community that covers a large part of the earth.

Arctic tundra is found at the top of the world around the North Pole. This land is known as the Arctic region. Alpine tundra is found at the tops of high mountains around the world.

Now You Know

Tundra comes from a Finnish word that means "land with no trees."

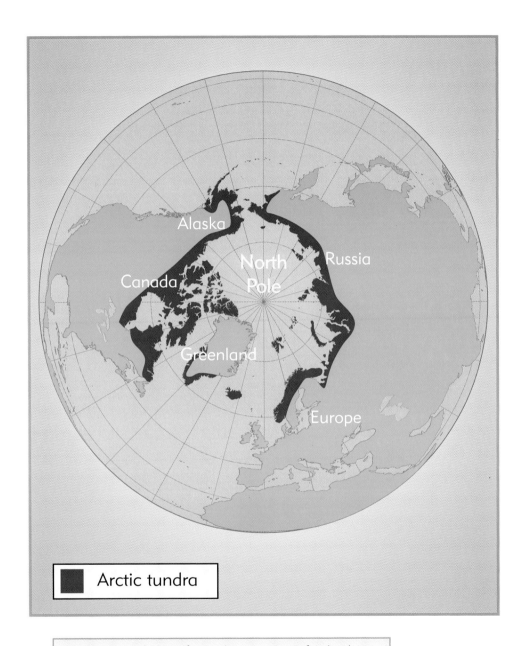

Arctic tundra

Arctic tundra is found in parts of Alaska, Canada, Greenland, Europe, and Russia.

Arctic Tundra

Winters in the arctic tundra are long, dark, and very cold. Summers are less than 60 days long. The ice in the top layer of soil melts in summer. This allows plants to grow and animals to find food.

Polar bears sleep close together for warmth in the cold arctic evenings.

Now You Know

Arctic tundra regions receive about 6 to 10 inches of rain or snowfall a year. This is less than the amount of rain that falls yearly on the deserts of North America.

Permafrost

Arctic tundra has permafrost. Permafrost is ground under the top layer of soil that remains frozen all year.

Plants and animals in the arctic tundra must be able to live in very cold weather. Arctic plants grow without much light and warmth. Arctic animals have babies before the cold winter comes. Some animals sleep through winter. Others move to warmer places during the coldest months.

Snow Bunting

Tundra birds, such as the snow bunting, often fly to warmer climates in the winter months.

Lichens

Lichens (LY-kuhnz) are small plants that often grow on rocks. Lichens grow very slowly. It is believed that some lichens are among the oldest living things on Earth.

Alpine Tundra

Alpine means "very high up." Alpine tundra can be found on mountains at 10,000 feet or higher. The ground is made of rock and soil. It is covered by snow 9 to 10 months of the year. Permafrost does not happen very often in alpine tundra regions. Plants grow closely together and near to the ground.

Wildflowers often grow in the alpine tundra during the summer.

Alpine tundra

Tree line

Alpine tundra temperatures can go from 60 degrees Fahrenheit (15 degrees Celsius) in daytime to below zero (–17 degrees Celsius) at night. Strong winds can reach 100 miles an hour.

Animals living in the alpine tundra have thick fur, feathers, or layers of fat. These help protect animals by keeping them warm in the cold weather.

Marmots are part of the squirrel family. They have thick fur to keep warm.

Mountain goats can easily travel across the rocky hills in the alpine tundra. They can jump more than 11 feet across the rocky land.

Living in the Tundra

People living in the tundra biome need to dress warmly. Clothes made from animal skins and fur protect people from cold temperatures and blowing winds.

There are few roads in the arctic tundra. People use dogsleds, snowmobiles, special trucks, and airplanes for travel.

The Inuit of Canada use animal skins to make watertight boots. They wear many layers of clothing to stay warm.

17

Today, many people who live in the alpine tundra are animal herders. Reindeer are raised for their milk, meat, and fur. Sheep are also raised there. Many hikers and climbers also enjoy visiting the alpine tundra.

In the summer, people hike in the high mountains of the alpine tundra.

Reindeer feed on tundra grasses, leaves, mosses, and lichens. They are trained to use their great strength to pull sleds.

1945559

The tundra biome is very cold, but many plants and animals are able to live there. The land, as well as the plants and animals of this biome, are easily hurt. People need to care for tundra regions so they continue to be a beautiful and healthy part of our world.

Litter and trash left in the tundra biome can last for many years. Rust from cans kills plants and is harmful to water.

Glossary

alpine tundra (al-**pyn** **tuhn**-druh) treeless, cold lands found at the tops of high mountains

arctic tundra (**ark**-tihk **tuhn**-druh) treeless, cold areas found around the North Pole, in parts of North America, Europe, and Asia

layer (**lay**-uhr) one thickness or level of something that is on top of another

permafrost (pur-muh-**frawst**) a layer of ground under the top layer of soil that remains frozen, preventing trees from growing

region (**ree**-juhn) any place or area on Earth

temperature (**tehm**-puhr-uh-chuhr) how hot or cold something is

Resources

Books

The Tundra
by Elizabeth Kaplan
Benchmark Books (1995)

Arctic Tundra: Land With No Trees
by Allan Fowler
Children's Press (1997)

Web Sites

Due to the changing nature of Internet links, PowerKids Press has developed an online list of Web sites related to the subject of this book. This site is updated regularly. Please use this link to access the list:

http://www.powerkidslinks.com/bio/tun/

Index

A

alpine tundra, 4–6,
    12–15, 18
animals, 8, 10, 14,
    20
arctic tundra, 4, 6–10,
    16

B

biome, 4–5, 16,
    20–21

L

layer, 8–9, 14, 17
lichens, 11, 19

N

North Pole, 6–7

P

permafrost, 9, 12
plants, 8, 10–12,
    20–21

R

reindeer, 18–19
region, 4, 6, 8,
    12, 20

Word Count: 412

Note to Librarians, Teachers, and Parents

If reading is a challenge, Reading Power is a solution! Reading Power is perfect for readers who want high-interest subject matter at an accessible reading level. These fact-filled, photo-illustrated books are designed for readers who want straightforward vocabulary, engaging topics, and a manageable reading experience. With clear picture/text correspondence, leveled Reading Power books put the reader in charge. Now readers have the power to get the information they want and the skills they need in a user-friendly format.